TROLL TALES

by ROBERT STEPHEN

illustrated by Rolf Lidberg

AULTON TROLLS

First published in 1999 *by*
AULTON TROLLS
An imprint of AULTON PRESS
Ardallie, Peterhead,
Scotland AB42 5BN

British Library Cataloguing in Publication Data
Stephen, Robert, 1949-
    Troll tales
    1. Trolls - Juvenile poetry 2. Children's poetry, English
    I. Title II. Lidberg, Rolf
    821. 9' 14

ISBN 0 - 9512459 - 3 - 7

Designed & Produced by Aulton Press
Typeset in Baskerville
Printed by The Bath Press, Glasgow

For Nuncles Tom, David, Sandy, Robbie and Robert

FOREWORD

This delightful book is the progeny of a deliciously unlikely collaboration between a Swedish troll-master (Rolf Lidberg) and a Scottish medical merman (Robert Stephen).

The Swedish troll-master is a gnarled, bearded, happy-go-lucky nature-lover and botanist, a specialist in his own right in orchids and fungi, who has delighted generations of Scandinavians with his witty, wry, enchanting drawings of ancient trolldom.

The Scottish medical merman is an offshore doctor from Peterhead, based in the Brent field halfway across the North Sea between Shetland and Norway. Occasionally he has to fly seriously ill or injured patients to hospital in Bergen. On one of these trips in 1995, he bought a handful of troll postcards at the airport. On the helicopter flight back offshore, he was enjoying the pictures "when a poem just came to me". This was *The Trolls and the Mermaid*, the prototype from which Dr Stephen developed his quirky vision of the 'Troll Country':

> 'And here the trolls live, strong and free,
> In peace with Nature's harmony;
> A rough-hewn, craggy, ancient race,
> More kind of heart than fair of face.
> The unkempt keepers of the land,
> From snowy peak to rocky strand;
> They know the hills, the streams, the lakes,
> The starry skies, the wooded brakes;
> They see the sunshine and the showers;
> They love the trees and all the flowers,
> The deer that run, the fish that swim,
> And every little bird that sings.'

In my own childhood, listening to tales from Icelandic folklore at my mother's knee, trolls were nothing like as amiable and environmentally correct creatures as those of Rolf Lidberg! Trolls were much more sinister beings, ogres one and all, monstrous and malignant, evil and ill-favoured. They lived in cliffs and preyed on any people unlucky enough to come within their reach. They hurled vast boulders around like pebbles and tore the legs off horses for a snack. A favourite Icelandic curse was 'The trolls take you!'

The world of trolls as seen by Rolf Lidberg and Robert Stephen is a much gentler, friendlier place. Your average troll, with his red nose and abundant beard, could be anybody's favourite eccentric uncle.

The raggedy troll children - the trollings - are as appealing and engaging a bunch of scamps as you could wish to find. Their little adventures in these pages have all the naïve charm of a long-lost world of natural innocence.

The illustrations are truly delightful, the ideas are alluring and some of the invented words are a joy - trollshop, trollcake and the irresistible trollipops.

'More kind of heart than fair of face' indeed. These *Troll Tales* are both droll tales and tall tales at the same time. They will bring pleasure to very, very many.

Magnus Magnusson K.B.E.

ACKNOWLEDGEMENTS

I should like to thank the troll-master himself, Rolf Lidberg, for his delightful paintings which have given us so much pleasure over the years, and without which the book could not have been written. I am particularly grateful for the two new illustrations he has kindly painted for us, and for the friendship of this remarkable man. Long may he flourish in the land of the trolls.

Thanks also to Alf and Ethel Hallén, Peter Åhl and all at Trollgalleriet for their friendship and hospitality, Hans Andersson of Trollrike for his photography, Rob Ward for his line drawings, Galvin and Dorrie Whitaker for their extensive knowledge of Scandinavian pickled herring, Mike Innes for his help with Alpine plants, and Willie for his many suggestions and (just occasionally) providing the right word.

Finally, as always, my thanks to Elizabeth, my wife, my valued adviser, my Solvi, for everything.

TROLL TALES   CONTENTS

TROLL COUNTRY - an introduction	PAGE 11
THE TROUT	PAGE 13
TROLLSHOP	PAGE 15
MOONLIGHT ENCOUNTER	PAGE 17
TROLL TALES	PAGE 19
THE TROLLS AND THE MERMAID	PAGE 21
TROLL MOON	PAGE 23
THE FISH-HOUSE	PAGE 25
CLOUDS	PAGE 27
THE FOREST LAKE	PAGE 29
COTTON GRASS	PAGE 33
THE SWING	PAGE 35
THE POACHERS' TALE	PAGE 37
THE FOREST-TROLL	PAGE 41
WHO WILL TAKE THE FIRST STEP?	PAGE 43
TROLLBOTANIST	PAGE 45
THE RAFT	PAGE 47
THE CRAYFISH	PAGE 49
THE FIDDLER'S TALE	PAGE 51
TROLLSTARS	PAGE 55
About the author	PAGE 56
About the artist	PAGE 57

TROLL TALES

TROLL COUNTRY

Beneath the lucid northern skies
A land of rugged mountains lies;
A land of shining waterfalls,
Of dizzy peaks and mountain walls;
Of lakes and tarns and sparkling rills
That flow down from the purple hills;
Of ancient forests, secret caves,
And sea cliffs pounded by the waves.

And here the trolls live, strong and free,
In peace with Nature's harmony;
A rough-hewn, craggy, ancient race,
More kind of heart than fair of face.
The unkempt keepers of the land,
From snowy peak to rocky strand:
They know the hills, the streams, the lakes,
The starry skies, the wooded brakes;
They see the sunshine and the showers;
They love the trees and all the flowers,
The deer that run, the fish that swim,
And every little bird that sings.

To pleasure (more than work) inclined,
And fiddle tunes and red troll wine,
They sing and dance and drink troll ale,
And drown their cares and tell troll tales.
And many tales are sung and told,
And legends of the days of old;
And some of these have come to men,
And so begins my story, friend.

THE TROUT

Will and Jill and Nuncle Bill
Went through the forest, up the hill.
Beneath the pine trees, dark and cool,
They found a secret gleaming pool
Where deer and squirrels come to drink,
And moss grows on the fountain's brink,
And tiny forest flowers peep out;
And there Will caught a speckled trout.
"*A splendid fish!*" his nuncle cried.
"We'll cook him by the waterside."
They made a fire and cooked the fish:
A sizzling, scrumptious, splendid dish.
"*Done to a turn!*" their nuncle said;
And a stoat ran off with the fish's head.
Then by the secret gleaming pool
Beneath the pine trees, dark and cool,
They sat them down and ate their fill,
Jill and Will and Nuncle Bill.

TROLLSHOP

Beneath the spreading chestnut tree,
Its wares displayed for all to see,
High on a hill the trollshop stands
And looks across the wooded lands.

There's sausages, salamis, hams;
Bread, coffee, sugar, pickles, jams;
Troll cheeses, trollcake, rich and sweet,
And all the things trolls like to eat;
And candles, matches, brushes, pails;
Ropes, needles, linen, hammers, nails;
And soap and fishing hooks and line,
And herrings packed in tubs of brine.

And here the trollfolk come to shop,
And meet old friends and sit and talk,
And catch up with the latest news,
And tell troll tales and air their views.
In little groups the trollwives chat:
"She *never!*" "*Did* she?" "Fancy that!"

Beneath the tree two nuncles smoke
And wag their heads and share a joke,
And talk about the olden days,
And criticise the modern ways.
Young lovers stand and shyly smile:
"I've really missed you for a while."
The trollings come for bags of sweets
And trollipops and other treats.
The trollshopkeeper knows them all,
From old grandmas to baby trolls.
In smart white coat and matching hat
He pauses for a friendly chat,
And as he packs their goods away
He shares the gossip of the day.

And so, beneath the chestnut tree,
The long day passes pleasantly.
Then in the evening's golden light
He shuts the trollshop for the night.

MOONLIGHT ENCOUNTER

A crescent moon shines in the West;
The quiet waters are at rest;
A footbridge spans the little stream
And alders frame the peaceful scene.
Rolf stands there in the silver light;
To fish the stream was his delight,
The solace of his childhood fears,
The joy of all his teenage years.

At first he never noticed her,
But gradually he was aware
That someone else was standing there;
Her perfume filled the evening air.
Annoyed at this unfair intrusion
Into his highly-prized seclusion,
He stared down at the stream below,
And checked his line, and watched the flow.

She knew he saw her standing there,
And sighed and tossed her golden hair.
"Caught anything?" he heard her say.
"No, nothing. Not a bite all day."
"A lovely moon tonight," said she.
"It's far too bright for fish," said he.
She moved a little closer then.
He fumbled with his line again.
Her fragrant perfume filled his head;
She touched his arm. "Poor thing," she said.
"You must be fed up here, alone.
Perhaps you'd like to walk me home?"

He walked her to her home that night.
And now his solace and delight,
His love, his joy beyond compare,
Is Solvi of the golden hair.

TROLL TALES

Close by the forest's shady eaves,
Beneath the tall and ancient trees,
A little house stands on the green
Beside the tumbling, laughing stream.
Behind the house a garden grows
With flowers and fruit and beans in rows;
And in the house are piles on piles
Of books and papers, scrolls and files.
And here, among the books and clutter,
Lives Nuncle Ben, the old woodcutter.

And he is learned in secret lore
And legends of the days before,
And stories of the ancient trees,
Of flowers and forests, birds and bees.
Troll children come from far and near
His thrilling stories for to hear.
His book he cradles on his knee,
Or on a mossy stump of tree,
And reads his tales with charm and wit,
While round his feet the trollings sit
Amazed, delighted, charmed, enthralled,
And listen to the tales unfold:

Of sun on leaf and wind on hill,
Of summer skies and winter's chill;
Of birdsong in the early spring,
And silver waters glimmering;
Of mountains, cold beneath the moon,
Where piping birds sing lonely tunes;
Of dwarves and goblins, elves and fays;
And legends of the elder days
When dragons prowled the northern lands
And grey ships sailed from elven strands;
Of troll kings, deep in mountain halls,
The Ancient Fathers of the trolls.

And there upon the summer green,
Beside the laughing, tumbling stream,
They listen till the tales are done,
Then off they wander, one by one,
To hearth and home, and so to bed,
Where dreams enfold each sleepy head,
Of sun on leaf and wind on hill,
Of summer skies and winter's chill . . .

THE TROLLS AND THE MERMAID

Over the hills and far away
Old Troll and his son went to fish one day.
They never found a fish at all,
But a pretty mermaid by a waterfall.
She sat beneath a leafy tree
And sang a song of the distant sea:
Of magic grottoes, secret caves,
And palaces beneath the waves;
Of coral gardens, rich and fair,
Where mermaids comb their golden hair;
Of many-coloured fish that flew
Through coral groves of deepest blue.
The pretty mermaid closed her song;
A sudden splash and she was gone.
Never a word spoke son nor troll,
Hushed by the lonely waterfall.

TROLL MOON

Over the hills and far away
The trolls and their children come to play.
When human folk are fast asleep
Out from the hidden woods they creep.
The trollfolk come from far and wide
To a grassy slope on the mountainside,
For the night that the troll moon shines is here,
The biggest feast in all the year.

The old tales tell when the earth was new,
And the mountains tall and the seas were blue,
And a full moon hung in the eastern sky,
The first trolls woke on the mountainside.
And the god of the mountain called them his own,
For he made them out of the rocks and stone;
And the young stars shone with an undimmed light
On an unstained world on the first troll night.
And they woke to the song of a nightingale
Who sang from a crag in the hidden vale.

So the trolls come back to the grassy slope
Each year on the night that the first trolls woke
To sing and to dance and to drink and to feast
Till the rising sun glows red in the East.

The trollfolk come from far and wide,
From wood and field and countryside.
There's young and old, and great and small,
And every different kind of troll:
Wood-trolls, hill-trolls, trolls from caves,
Sea-trolls with voices like the waves,
Old lady trolls wrapped up in shawls,
And trolls from deepest mountain halls.
The band strikes up the old troll tunes
As they wait for the rising of the moon.
They sing and dance around the fire
While the fiddles shriek higher and higher;
Troll children laugh and clap for glee;
And the red troll wine flows fast and free.

The music stops as a bugle shrills
And the moon peeps over the eastern hills;
The mountains ring with a mighty cheer
As the troll moon rises high and clear.
The band strikes up the old troll tunes
And they dance in the light of the rising moon.
They dance and feast till the break of day,
Over the hills and far away.

THE FISH-HOUSE

Upon an old and creaking quay
Between the village and the sea,
Behind the rocks that guard the vik,
The battered wooden fish-house sits.

Troll fishers work the sound all night;
And in the early morning light
They row ashore to land the catch:
Cod, haddock, mackerel, herrings, sprats.

The boats row through the open door
And tie up to the fish-house floor.
The fish are cleaned and packed in trays,
Then cured in *many* different ways:
Some are dried and some are smoked
Over smouldering chips of oak;
But most are packed in kegs of brine
To keep them for the wintertime.

There's sur sill, kryddsill, gravad lax,
Rökt böckling, trollsill, tubs of sprats;
Salt cod, senapssill, sherrysill,
Surströmming, eels, and sill i dill;
And hundreds more than I can say
(The list would take your breath away).

All summer long they cure the catch
In tubs and barrels, kegs and vats,
To last them till the winter's done
(For trolls eat herrings by the *ton*),
Till frosty days are at an end
And summer's blossom comes again.

CLOUDS

The day is warm, the clouds are high
Against an azure depth of sky;
Upon the grass lies Father Troll
And, stretched beside him, little Moll.
The fragrant turf smells warm and sweet;
Soft leaves caress her shoeless feet.

They lie there in the meadow grass
And watch the summer clouds drift past:
Immense, high-towering, jagged, curled;
Cloud-symbols of a magic world.
Each looks for what the other sees:
High mountains, valleys, rivers, trees;
Or towers and castles, tall and fair,
And folds and curls of angel's hair;
Cliffs and forests, hills and caves,
Sea-islands washed by silver waves;
And stately galleons sailing by
Across the ocean of the sky.

The ever-shifting vapours change
Into outlines new and strange:
A jester with his cap and bells,
Armed men and hooded sentinels;

Wild horses running, proud and free,
Across a silver-dappled sea;
And many-pillared cloudy halls,
And heroes, feasts and festivals;
Huge dragons breathing fire and smoke,
And unicorns, and elven folk:
Cloud-maidens clad in misty veils,
And bearded warriors, tall and pale;
And Heimdall with his mighty horn,
High on the rainbow's shining form.

And sometimes, clear against the sky,
They see a great white horse go by,
His coat as pure as driven snow,
And silver wings that flash and glow;
Creator of the enchanted stream,
The source of all that poets dream.

Upon the meadow grass they lie
And watch the pageant of the sky,
And listen to the lark that thrills
The green earth with his heaven-born trills,
Till little Moll is fast asleep
And Father Troll is snoring deep.

THE FOREST LAKE

One morning early little Fred
Crept downstairs from his cosy bed.
He'd hardly slept a wink that night
And woke up long before daylight,
For Nuncle Ned would come and take
Him fishing on the Forest Lake.
He'd never caught a fish before.
A gentle tap came to the door,
And on the step stood Nuncle Ned.
"A perfect day for trout," he said.

The early morn was calm and still;
They took the path across the hill.
Some stars still twinkled in the blue;
The morning fields were wet with dew.
Then down the forest track they went,
The dark air heavy with the scent
Of sticky resin, sharp and sweet;
Pine needles rustled at their feet.

They reached the placid Forest Lake
Just as the dawn began to break.
They saw the splendid morning glow
Reflected in the lake below;

The air was still with not a sound,
The silent forest all around.
"It's awful quiet, Nuncle Ned."
"Ah, not for long," his nuncle said.
And then a single blackbird spoke
And all the woodland chorus broke:
The chaffinch, robin and the wren,
The warblers, thrushes, doves and then
The red sun peeped above the trees
And waters riffled in the breeze.

"We'll make our camp down by the bay
And brew some tea to start the day.
Go fetch some twigs and bring them here
While I set up the fishing gear."
They drank their tea around the fire
And listened to the forest choir.
A trout splashed and the ripples spread.
"It's time to start," said Nuncle Ned.

He showed Fred how to bait for trout,
And hold the rod, and cast it out.
"You'll be all right here in this bay;
I'll try the point across the way."

All morning long they fished the lake;
But never a bite, never a take.
Said Nuncle Ned, "That's awful queer;
I *know* there's plenty fish in here.
We'll have some lunch and then we'll see.
I think we'll try the sunken tree;
It's over by the reedy bay;
I had *five* trout from there one day."

They fished with bait, they fished with flies;
But never a strike, never a rise.
They tried it out, they tried it in;
But never a scale, never a fin.
They fished until the evening light;
But never a take, never a bite.
The sun went down; the West grew red.
The old troll yawned and scratched his head.
"I'll go and light the fire," said he,
"And put the kettle on for tea.
I've never seen the lake like this:
A whole day gone and not a fish."

But little Fred cast out his line.
"I'm going to try just one more time.
I thought I saw a fish," said he,
"Across there by the sunken tree."
His nuncle smiled and shook his head.
"All right, but don't be long," he said.
Out on the surface of the lake
The whorls of mist began to snake.
Fred stood there in the fading light
When suddenly his line ran tight;
His rod bent down; he gave a shout:
"Quick! Nuncle Ned, I've got a trout!"

Old Nuncle Ned came puffing back.
"Hold up your rod! Don't give him slack;
He'll wrap you round the sunken tree.
That's quite a fish, my lad," said he.
The big trout dived and fought and splashed,
But young Fred got it in at last.
His nuncle bent and scooped it out.
"Well done, young Fred! A splendid trout!"

With triumph shining in his eyes
He carried back his gleaming prize:
A splendid brown trout in its prime
Smelt sweet and fresh like mountain thyme,
With yellow flanks and olive back,
And stippled spots of red and black.
They laid the rods against a tree,
And by the fire they ate their tea.
"I'm sleepy now," yawned little Fred.
The old troll tucked him into bed.
He hugged his trout and dozed away
With memories of his happy day:
The stars, the sky, the lake, the trees,
The birds, the sun, the morning breeze.

COTTON GRASS

Beneath the rain-washed northern skies
A land of placid waters lies;
A magic land of singing rushes,
Of silver pools and myrtle bushes;
Between the forest and the river,
Where kingcups glow and sedges quiver,
And curlews call and wild duck nest;
It's there the cotton grass grows best.

And there, when summer nights are young,
The trollwives and their children come,
Before the eastern stars are bright,
Beneath the evening's golden light
When mists enfold the sleeping marsh,
To pluck the fluffy cotton grass.

The trollfolk wander to and fro
Among the fields of summer snow,
By forest's edge and reedy pool,
Until their bulging sacks are full
Of cotton grass to spin the yarn
To weave the clothes to keep them warm
When nights are long and days are chill
And winter snow lies on the hill.

THE SWING

Above the village, on the slope,
There stands a gnarled and ancient oak
From where the views stretch far and wide
To wood and field and mountainside;
And down below the river runs,
Bright waters sparkling in the sun.

And here, on many a summer's day,
The village trollings come to play
And while away the sunny hours:
They climb the trees, they gather flowers;
They look for tracks of deer and fox,
And blow the dandelion clocks;
They picnic on the summer grass
And watch the fluffy clouds sail past.
But better far than all these things
Is playing on the wooden swing:
To swing up in the air so high,
To soar like birds up in the sky,
To see the shining river flow
And fields and forests far below,
And feel the dizzy rush of air,
Is happiness beyond compare.

One summer's morning little Flo
Climbed up the slope with Nuncle Joe;
He'd come to push her on the swing
And see what else was happening.
He gently swung her to and fro;
The old troll smiled to watch her go.
"When I was young and fit," said he,
"I had a swing upon a tree.
I used to swing for hours on end;
I'd like to try it once again."

The trollings cheered with one accord
To watch the old troll climb aboard.
"Be careful, please," said little Flo.
"I'll be all right," said Nuncle Joe.
At first he kept close to the ground
(Smiles and laughter all around),
But as he got the hang of things
Higher and higher flew the swing;
And higher still they watched it go.
"That's plenty now!" said little Flo.

But Nuncle Joe was having fun
And wouldn't stop for anyone.
The wide-eyed trollings stood and gasped
Each time old Joe went whooshing past;
They'd never seen a swing so high;
It seemed to reach up to the sky.
The branches shuddered on the tree;
The old troll yelled and whooped for glee.
The ancient bough began to crack;
It parted with a fearsome *snap!*
And through the air they watched him fly.
"I never thought he'd go *that high!*"
He shrieked and soared into the blue,
Then curved and disappeared from view
Behind the shoulder of the hill.
The morning air was calm and still.

The trollings searched the slope below,
But not a sign of Nuncle Joe.
And little Flo began to cry,
"I told him not to go so high."
Then from a bush they heard a shout:
"I'm over here! Please help me out!"
He'd landed in a clump of gorse:
Bumped, bruised and scratched, but nothing worse.
At last the trollings got him down
And cheered him through the little town:
The hero, loved by one and all,
Old Nuncle Joe, the flying troll.

THE POACHERS' TALE

Beneath tree shadows, dark and cool,
Which lie across the midnight pool
There comes the sound of dipping oars
Which slowly pass from shore to shore.
Dark ripples spread across the flow
And voices murmur, soft and low;
A gently bobbing line of floats
Curves out behind the little boat.

They reach the other side at last.
"That's us," said Hans. "I'll make her fast."
"Well don't be long," said Franz." And watch!
Don't make a noise among the rocks."
Franz sat and waited nervously;
Hans tied the net up to a tree.
"Right, that's her fast; let's go," said Hans.
"*Quick!* Get aboard and row," said Franz.

And back across the pool they row;
A fish splashed in the run below.
Said Hans, "The fish are here all right;
We're going to fill our boots tonight!"
"Shh! Keep it down, you silly goat!
Let's get ashore and hide the boat."

They pulled the boat behind a tree;
Franz scanned the river anxiously.
"There's something funny here tonight."
"*Come on,*" said Hans. "We'll be all right."

They settled down to wait and watch,
Then something in the river splashed.
"*A fish!*" cried Hans. "A good one too;
Right in the net. No, wait: *there's two!*"
Another, then another struck;
The pair could not believe their luck.
Out in the pool the salmon splashed;
They felt the cork-line pull and snatch.
Now even Franz was filled with glee.
"We'd better get her hauled," said he.
"I've never seen a catch like this:
We'll sink the boat with weight of fish!"

With half the net to come or more,
Two dozen salmon on the floor,
And twenty pounds the smallest fish,
The little boat began to list.

Then suddenly a blinding light
Lit up the blackness of the night:
The river-watchers, unawares,
Had crept up on the hapless pair.
"We've got you now! Game's up!" they cried.
"Just pull in slowly to the side."

"Quick, Franz, *your knife!* Before they come.
We'll shoot the falls; *let's cut and run!"*
"Not in the dark!" cried Franz in fright.
"You'll never shoot the falls at night."
But Hans worked quickly with the knife.
"That's us!" he cried. *"Row for your life!*
They'll never follow us down there:
I know these falls; they wouldn't dare."
The little boat shot down the pool.
The watchers yelled, *"Come back, you fools!"*

"We'll never make it through," said Franz.
"I'll keep you right; *just row!"* said Hans.
"I shot these rapids once before;
Keep close beside the wooded shore,
Then when you see white water gleam
Head for the middle of the stream."
By now the stream was deep and fast;
The rocky banks went rushing past;

They heard the torrent's awful roar.
"Keep closer to the wooded shore!"
"I can't! The current's got her now!"
"Look out! There's rocks below the bow!"
A sickening *crunch* of wood on stone;
The boat reared up, then she was gone.

A mile below the falls or more,
Our heroes struggled to the shore.
They shook with cold, they shook with fear;
They'd lost their boat, they'd lost their gear.
Half-drowned, exhausted, pale and wan,
They trudged home in the early dawn.

And that was twenty years ago.
Now they no longer poaching go.
But sometimes, round their winter ale,
When nuncles tell their fishy tales
Of rods and lines and flies and hooks,
Of winter floods and summer brooks;
And all the giant fish they've caught,
And bigger ones they almost got;
They tell the disbelieving trolls
About the night they shot the falls.

THE FOREST -TROLL

His hair is red like autumn leaves;
His limbs are gnarled like ancient trees;
His eyes are blue like summer seas.

Like cherry bark his skin is brown;
Like lichen fronds his beard hangs down,
His mouth more apt to smile than frown.

His merry face is kind and good;
His laughter, like a brook in flood,
Rings through the arches of the wood.

You'll find him in the leafy shade,
Or walking in the sunlit glade,
Or by the Forest River laid,

Where, in the drowsy heat of noon
When crickets sing and turtles croon,
He takes his pipe and blows a tune.

And when the evening star declines
You'll find him stretched beneath the pines;
On mossy bed his length reclines.

And sometimes when the night is old,
Beneath the pale stars shining cold,
You'll find him on the empty wold.

He loves to see the morning rise,
And hail the dawn with cheerful eyes,
And drink the splendour of the skies.

He knows the trees and marks their growth
From acorn shoots to mighty oaks;
From heathland scrub to hazel copse.

He hears the trees and loves them well,
And listens to the tales they tell
In gloomy shade and sunny dell.

From summer's sun to winter's freeze
He's walked his wood for centuries,
The ancient keeper of the trees.

But passers-by may only see
A gnarled and hoary, moss-hung tree
Amid the lusher greenery.

WHO WILL TAKE THE FIRST STEP?

They both forgot how it began,
But now it was quite out of hand.
If he said *"Black!"* then she'd say *"White!"*
If she said *"Wrong!"* then he'd say *"Right!"*
She said she couldn't understand
Why he'd not meet her just demands.
He said, *"I've never liked that dress."*
She said, *"You're always such a mess."*
She dragged up old hurts from the past.
He said, *"It wasn't meant to last."*

And to and fro they passed the blame
Like rallies in a tennis game;
Both hurting more than they'd admit,
But never giving in a bit.
At last they argued to a halt,
And, back to back, they stood and sulked.

Long time they stood upon the hill.
The sky grew dark, the wind blew chill;
They heard the trees begin to roar;
The heavens opened and it poured.

She shivered. "Could you hold me near?"
He held her close. "I'm sorry, dear."
They stood there in the pouring rain
And kissed and made it up again.

When pride is hurt and tempers fray
We all say things we shouldn't say,
And take positions quite absurd
When *sorry* is the hardest word.
But life is short, too short to spend
In fighting with your dearest friend;
So put your hurts and pride away,
Forgive each other while you may,
For love's a sweet and precious thing,
And who knows what tomorrow brings?

TROLLBOTANIST

He walks the country far and wide,
By lake and stream and woodland ride,
From sheltered field and lowland hedge
To grassy slope and dizzy edge.
From mountain-top to rocky strand,
With well-thumbed book and glass in hand,
From dawn to dusk he spends his hours
Among his precious norland flowers.

He sees the morning's splendour rise
When Dawn illumes the eastern skies;
In matchless shades of rose and gold
He sees her fiery robes unfold.
He marks the lark upon the wing
And loves to hear the linnet sing,
The blackbird fluting from the thorn,
And every bird that hails the morn.

Beneath the trees he stands and stares
And savours the sweet morning air,
Where downy rose and eglantine
Their deep and fragrant scents combine.
And every plant he loves and knows,
Each leaf that shines, each flower that glows:

Bluebells and wood anemones;
Red poppies dancing in the breeze;
Bright orchid flowers of rarest hue;
Heartsease, and roses soft with dew;
Tall foxgloves, purple on their stems,
And lilies crowned with diadems;
Sweet cicely, the norland myrrh,
Adorned with silver gossamer.

Sometimes he seeks the mountain flowers
By craggy ledge and granite towers:
Wild thyme, sea pink, moss campion;
Roseroot, crowfoot, spiked rampion;
Cranesbill and alpine meadow rue;
Forget-me-nots of brightest blue;
And, fairest of them all by far,
The rare and lovely alpine star.

Too soon the happy hours fly past.
He gathers up his things at last
And homeward turns to dine and rest;
The sun sinks in the crimson West.

THE RAFT

The twilight deepened into night
And in the East the stars grew bright.
The quiet evening breeze had died;
The young moon slanted down the sky.
A peace lay over wood and hill;
The waters of the lake were still.
A little rustic houseboat lay
At anchor in the tree-lined bay;
A family of mountain-trolls
Had left their many-caverned halls
And come to spend their autumn break
Upon the peaceful upland lake.

All day they'd played upon the shore:
They rowed, they fished, they swam, explored;
Picked berries on the purple hill,
And picnicked by a sparkling rill.
They rowed back through the evening's gold
And watched the sunset clouds unfold.

They lit the fire and cooked their tea.
The troll twins nodded sleepily.
Mum tucked the trollings into bed
And kissed each golden sleepyhead.
"Goodnight, my loves. Sleep deep and warm.
Sweet dreams, my darlings, till the morn."
Old Father Troll sat by the fire;
The kettle sang; he yawned. "I'm tired.
We'll have another cup of tea
And watch the moon go down," said he.
Their supper done, to bed they creep,
By gentle waves soon rocked asleep.
The moon slept in her hilly bed;
The bright stars twinkled overhead.

THE CRAYFISH

A summer's night, the moon is full;
It shines on forest, rock and pool;
And down beside the little stream,
Beneath the trees a lantern gleams.

Says Father Troll, "Now here's the plan:
Wade slow, and softly as you can.
You'll find them in the weedy bits,
Just poke round gently with your sticks;
Or in the rocks, that's where they stay;
Beneath the stones they hide all day.
Be careful now; if you're not quick
They'll give you quite a nasty nip.
It's best to hold them by the back;
It's easy once you've got the knack.
For catching crayfish all you need
Is stealth, agility and speed."

They spread out up and down the stream
And to and fro their torches gleam.
Upon the shore Troll Mother stays
And boils the pot to cook the crays.
They wander up and down the pool;
And soon the steaming pot is full
Of crayfish, juicy, fat and sweet.
"They're ready now," cried Mum. *"Let's eat."*

Then from the stream: "I'm coming, dear.
I've got a *giant* crayfish here;
I've nearly got him from his hole.
I won't be long," cried Father Troll.
Then Father Troll let out a scream
And leapt and danced about the stream.
He howled and yowled: *"It's got my toe!*
Do something, quick! It won't let go!"
"Just stealth, agility and speed",
Laughed Mother Troll; "that's all you need."
He hopped and jigged; he screeched and screamed,
Then tripped and landed in the stream.

He spluttered to the waterside;
The trollings laughed until they cried.
"It's easy when you've got the knack!"
"It's best to hold them by the back!"
Troll Father rubbed his toe and frowned
(Hoots of laughter all around).
"It could be worse, I might suppose",
Said Mum: "it could have been your nose!"

They still remember, one and all,
The night the cray caught Father Troll.

THE FIDDLER'S TALE

The winter's night was cold and bleak
With stinging showers of hail and sleet;
But in the village hostelry
The talk and ale were flowing free.
With song and dance and sprightly tune
The merry hours passed all too soon.
The fiddler left the cheery inn,
Well-fortified with ale and gin.

The wind howled through the naked trees;
The old man struggled through the breeze
With hood pulled up and head bent low.
He still had many miles to go
To where his little cottage stood;
His way lay through the Old Troll Wood.

Beneath the trees the night was black;
He heard the branches groan and crack;
He heard the tempest howl and moan.
At last he reached the Old Troll Stone;
A looming presence in the dark,
The Old Stone was the halfway mark.
He felt great weariness assail;
His aching legs began to fail.

Another hour and he'd be home;
He roused himself and struggled on.
But sleepiness was all around;
It seemed to rise up from the ground.
It filled his eyes, it filled his head;
His stumbling feet like lumps of lead.
"I need to rest a while," said he.
"I'll lie down here against this tree."
He leaned against its ancient bole
As over him sweet slumber stole.

He woke up with a sudden start;
The woody air was warm and dark.
He felt about him fearfully
And knew: he was *inside* the tree.
Inside the tree! O dreadful doom!
He peered about him in the gloom.
And then he saw the faintest glow;
It seemed to come up from below.
A glow? a light? inside the tree?
He moved towards it cautiously.
He stood amazed at what he'd found:
A passageway led underground.

And then sweet sounds his ear beguiled:
A haunting music, strange and wild;
It trilled and echoed in the depths.
The road led down with many steps.
He started down, afraid but drawn;
The haunting music led him on.
Down stairs and slopes the passage wound,
Deeper and deeper underground,
By crooked paths and secret ways;
The strange glow lit the old man's face.
The lilting strains grew louder still;
He stepped in time; his heart was thrilled.
The passage opened out at last
And through a carven arch he passed.

He found himself in a Great Hall
With multitudes of dancing trolls:
Fat ones, thin ones, great and small;
Young ones, old ones, short and tall;
They stepped, they jigged, they reeled and whirled;
They kicked, they leapt, they whooped and skirled;
While at the tables round the walls,
With jugs of ale, sat ancient trolls;
And in an alcove by the stairs
Troll fiddlers played their reels and airs.

A young troll maiden, fair and sweet,
Appeared and led him to a seat.
"Welcome! We've been expecting you.
I hear you play the fiddle too."
The old man blushed and bowed. "My dear,
I've played the fiddle for many a year,
From summer's sun to winter's gloom,
But *never* have I heard such tunes."

The music played; the trollfolk danced;
The fiddler sat as in a trance.
It played a song he seemed to know,
But lost somewhere, long, long ago.
The melodies would shift and change,
Weaving patterns new and strange:
The song of birds, wind in the trees;
The laughing brook, the rolling seas;
The thunder's growl, the tempest's roar;
Lake waters lapping on the shore;
The gentle sound of summer rain;
It healed his heart and eased his pain.

For many hours (or was it days?)
He listened to the music play.
The young troll maiden came again;
He knew the night was at an end.
The music stopped. She smiled. "It's time
To say goodbye. I brought some wine."

The red troll wine was rich and warm,
Full-bodied, deep; he drained the horn.
He drifted in its pleasant glow
And heard a peaceful music flow.
It lifted him as on a breeze;
He floated over golden seas
And silver waves that broke and curled
Upon the margins of the world.

He woke beneath the naked trees;
The dead leaves fluttered in the breeze;
The early dawn was bleak and chill;
A fox barked on the distant hill.
He walked home in the growing light
And pondered all he'd seen that night;
The night he'd been in the Great Hall
And heard the music of the trolls.

TROLLSTARS

Deep in the stillness of the night
The northern stars shine clear and bright
Upon the peaceful scene below:
The silent land is deep in snow,
And on his footsleigh Nuncle Bill
Is homeward bound with little Will.

He'd never seen so many stars.
"Please, Nuncle, tell me what they are,
And why they only shine at night,
Why some are red and some are white,
And some are still, some shine like flames.
Who made the stars? Who gave them names?"

Bill smiled, "For years I've watched the sky;
Like you, I often wonder why.
But still, I'll tell you what I know.
It's stars that twinkle; planets glow.
You see that red one over there?
That's Tyr, the ancient god of war.
Frey's Sickle swings around the Pole,
The Guiding Star of sailor trolls;
Thor with his shining belt of steel;
And Garm, the hellhound, at his heel.

And Balder, herald of the morn,
You'll find him high above the dawn;
Or when the sun has gone to rest
He lingers in the crimson West."
And then a strange and wondrous sight
Lit up the darkness of the night:
The ever-changing Northern Dawn,
The Valkyrs' Banners, glowed and shone
Like fiery curtains, splendid flowers;
In silent awe they gazed for hours.

The colours faded and were gone.
But in the East, above the dawn,
A single star shone clear and bright;
It seemed a pure and holy light.
"There's Balder in the East!" said Will.
"Well done, my lad!" said Nuncle Bill.
"We'll soon be home, then off to bed;
I see the village lights ahead."

They reached the village on the slope,
And in their hearts shone joy and hope.
The first rays of the sun felt warm
That splendid foremost Christmas morn.

ABOUT THE AUTHOR

Robert Stephen comes from the North East of Scotland's fisher folk and has already made a name for himself as a successful poet and storyteller with three Scottish best sellers.

He was a fisherman for a year before studying at Aberdeen University and graduating M.A. then M.B. Ch.B. Now, while working as a doctor on the North Sea oil rigs, Robert has written his first troll book. He became interested in Rolf Lidberg's troll paintings after finding them at Bergen Airport as postcards, having escorted a seriously ill patient there.

Living in a croft in Buchan with his wife, Elizabeth, and many animals, Robert is surrounded by the things he loves: trees, wild plants, skies and stars, from which he draws much of the inspiration for his poetry.

He also has a great passion for the sea, whether he is sailing, fishing, or exploring the underwater landscape.

He is currently working on another troll book in collaboration with Rolf Lidberg.